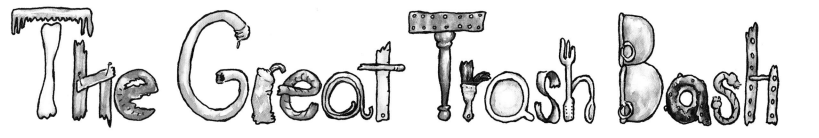

The Great Trash Bash

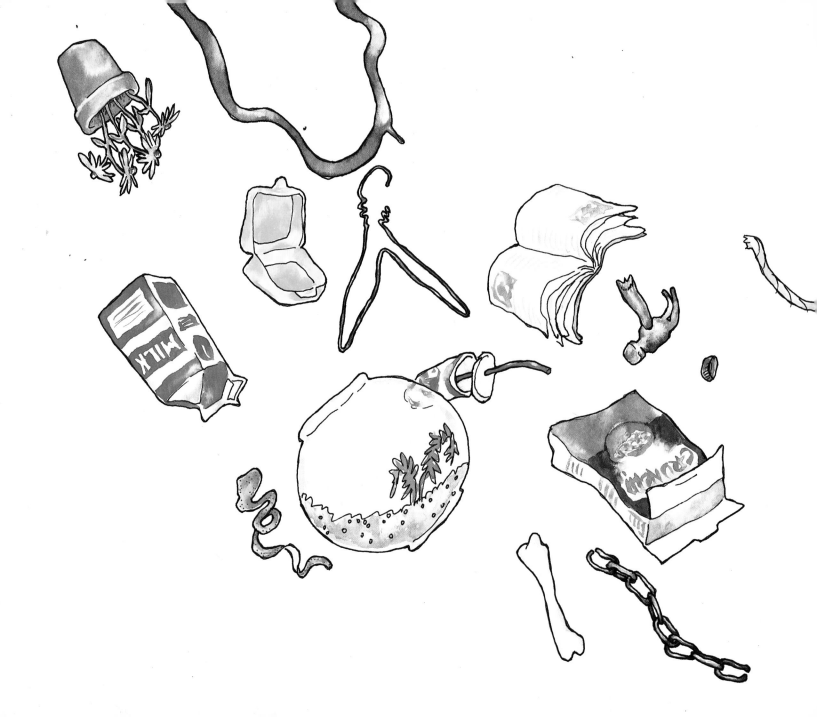

The Great Trash Bash

LOREEN LEEDY

Holiday House / New York

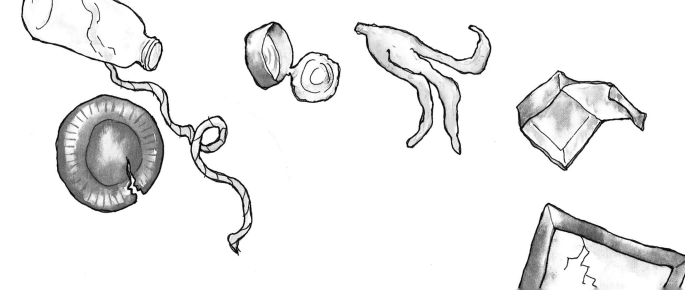

To trash-bashers everywhere

Library of Congress Cataloging-in-Publication Data
Leedy, Loreen.
The great trash bash / by Loreen Leedy.—1st ed.
p. cm.
Summary: The animal citizens of Beaston discover better ways to
recycle and control their trash.
ISBN 0-8234-0869-8
[1. Litter (Trash)—Fiction.   2. Refuse and refuse disposal—
Fiction.   3. Recycling (Waste, etc.)—Fiction.   4. Pollution—
Fiction.   5. Animals—Fiction.] I. Title.
PZ7.L51524Gr 1991   90-46554   CIP   AC
[E]—dc20
ISBN 0-8234-0869-8
ISBN 0-8234-1634-8 (pbk.)

WELCOME TO BEASTON

There are rolling hills and wiggly roads and shady trees in Beaston. It is a home to any animal that can run, fly or swim. But something is wrong.

The mayor is searching for an answer.

He talks to citizens wherever he goes.

At last, Mayor Hippo finds the answer.

To find out more about trash, the mayor goes to the dump.

Next, he visits the incinerator.

The landfill is the last stop.

Mayor Hippo calls a town meeting.

At the meeting, the animals think of ways to solve the trash problem. They start to make changes in their everyday life.

Citizens take out their tools.

They start to clean up Beaston.

They even find some good uses for trash.

Soon, the town opens a recycling center.

In the recycling center, the trash is sorted out.

There are rolling hills and wiggly roads and shady trees in Beaston. It is a home to any animal that can run, fly or swim. Beaston is a beautiful place.

HERE ARE SOME IDEAS FOR CUTTING DOWN ON TRASH:

1. Use dishes instead of disposable cups and plates.
2. Keep junk mail for scrap paper.
3. Buy products made from recycled materials.
4. Avoid buying products with several layers of packaging.
5. Repair broken items instead of buying new ones.
6. Buy beverages in returnable bottles.
7. Reuse a large envelope by attaching a new address label.
8. Save glass, metal, paper, cartons, and plastic to recycle.
9. Pick up litter on roadsides.
10. Encourage parents to use cloth diapers—(disposable diapers fill up landfills).
11. Donate extra clothes and toys to charity.
12. Buy new products only if you really need them.
13. Don't waste paper. Write on both sides.